In the Old Language…
 following the path of the Poet
Copyright © 2020 by Helen Morrissey Rizzuto
ISBN 978-0-578-76679-9

Poems, prose extracts and interior photographs copyright © 2007, 2020 by Helen Morrissey Rizzuto

Cover:
Heaven's Gates
Ciaran McHugh

The cover is a photograph of the old wrought iron gates at the entrance to the Glen at Knocknarea. The Glen (also known as the Alt) is a dramatic chasm on the southern slopes of Knocknarea mountain in Co. Sligo, featured in the poem The Man and the Echo by W. B. Yeats.

Unfortunately, after posing as sentries to the Glen for probably more than two centuries, the gates featured in this photograph were stolen in July 2011. It is unsettling to think that these iconic cultural landmarks which provided such a tangible connection to Yeats in Sligo (he would have walked through them) have in all likelihood been sold as scrap metal.
 Ciaran McHugh

In the Old Language...
following the path of the poet

poems, prose and photographs
inspired at the Yeats International Summer School
Sligo

Helen Morrissey Rizzuto

Also by Helen Morrissey Rizzuto

<u>POETRY</u>

Evening Sky On a Japanese Screen

A Bird in Flight

in the dark curfew'd streets
Long Beach, Long Island in the aftermath…

The Lenten Moon

<u>NONFICTION</u>

American By Choice, One Man's Journey
with Alfredo Fuentes, former Battalion Chief F.D.N.Y,
Survivor of the 9/11 attacks on the World Trade Center

Acknowledgments

In the writing of any book, even the smallest of tomes, there exists a host of influences, and more people than one can adequately thank for the unique way in which they contribute to the creation of the work; thus, this list remains, at best, a partial one.

To my family whose love and support are uncompromising and incomparable and who make each work possible.

With gratitude to Annie Scavo, Miriam Polli Katsikis and Kathy Melia Levine for the lifelong gift of their friendship, and my equally lifelong writing partners Hilari Cohen, Niki Petruzzi, Joan Dupre and Ellen Greenfield for their encouragement and willingness to explore and to challenge me to unearth the word from the dream. Mary Garrity and Paula Christman, while no longer physically among us, remain no less a part of this wise group of friends.

With gratitude to the cartographers who plotted my trip to Sligo, the trip down to Limerick and all places in between, and made the journey an unforgettable one, Virginia Madden and Rev. Derek Meskell, CSsR.

To Professors Kevin Murphy and the late George Watson for the warmth they showed a stranger in a strange and beautiful land.

To Richard who inspired, Gerald who insisted, and Grace who brings all things together, and to Declan who is fluent in the old language and who lights the way through its dim and ancient passages with the flame of possibility, a heartfelt thank you.

Dedication

for Bill Ochs, friend and teacher who introduced
me to the beauty, joy, sadness and history of
Ireland through her earliest language, her music

and as always, for my family

CONTENTS

PROSE

POEMS

PHOTOGRAPHS

Introduction

We enter a lighted theatre. People are being shown to their seats, and soon a warning bell will sound. Final coughs are coughed, cell phones are turned off and tucked away, and bags slipped under seats. The lights dim, and the curtain rises on a stage that holds a single chair, a bare table and a window bearing a steady rain. We are drawn to the window and the rain. In those few moments, before a word is uttered, we have entered a world within a world, a world apart from the one in which we live, in which we sit.

The philosopher Gaston Bachelard, in *The Poetics of Space*, states, "when a relaxed spirit meditates and dreams, immensity seems to expect images of immensity. The mind sees and continues to see *objects*, while the spirit finds the *nest of immensity* in an object" ... or *place*, one might say (italics mine). This immensity opens up around one like a many-chambered mansion; the more deeply one explores and allows what is there to grow inside the imagination, the more one sees.

In an earlier unpublished version of *In the Old Language...* titled *A Sligo Journal*, I didn't set out to prove the truth of Bachelard's statement, I didn't set out to do anything but record my impressions of a place that had been the cherished childhood summer home of a favorite poet. It was a means of documenting the time that I had spent at the Yeats International Summer School, and yet, as I gathered materials from that period for this work, I discovered an entire file – sketches, character studies, poems, stories and chapters. A process that had taken seed had begun to flourish, without my realizing. Over the years, in between the writing of those first poems and the years of writing, publishing and teaching that followed, it seems I had never stopped writing about Sligo. Bachelard would not have been surprised, nor would Yeats. It was his path that led me there.

One does not presume to know William Butler Yeats, in spite of knowledge imparted by erudite scholars like Professors Helen Vendler, Maureen Murphy and the late George Watson, my instructors at the Yeats International Summer School in 2007, who inspired further research and study and ... *dreaming*, to use Bachelard's term. Yeats is like that road that stretches out before one and leads through city, countryside, up into dark mountainous regions and into small cottages lit only by fire and the warmth and chill of stories lived and told there – like those other unexplored "caverns measureless to man" as Coleridge described them in all their dual interiority.

The journey is an endless one, which makes it intriguing and exciting, but also, because it is Yeats, exacting. The *Old Language* of the title of this work therefore, requires a little clarification. It is not Gaelic or Old Irish. Whenever Yeats was asked why he did not write in Gaelic, his response was that while Gaelic was his national tongue, it was not his mother tongue. That, he explained, was English. The *Old Language* of this book's title refers not only to the earlier and earliest languages spoken, but also to the language of all those who ever lived in this place, who seemed to disappear at death, but did not. The dead, Yeats suggested, were believed "to have stayed where they had lived, or near it, [they] sought no abstract region of blessing or punishment, but retreated, as it were, into the hidden character of their neighborhood."*

That then is the *Old Language* referenced here. It is the language that existed, and continues to exist, in the earth and of the earth, among those who reside in a land long after they're thought gone, a language more inclusive than Gaelic, Old Irish, English, more inclusive than that language spoken by the peasants up in the hills who provided Lady Gregory and William Butler Yeats the foundation of some of their more famous works. It is the language of the fauna, flora and the spirit of every rock, blade of grass, storm cloud and turned over plot of dirt. That is the language – the *underpainting* – of this small collection.

---

*A General Introduction for my Works – 1937 [unpub] reprinted from Essays and Introductions London, Macmillan, 1961.

in the Beginning...

The land must have been conceived in Night, before thought gave rise to creation. Even now, too much about the place points to the hours of darkness, the hours of sleeplessness and doubt, abandonment and embrace, those hours when earth struggles with the firmament, or is content to rest in its arms.

In the old language, the place was called Sligeach. You pursed your lips and whispered "Shhhhh... shhhh... shleeg... ah," and the sound was that of river water, like the water that has flowed through this land for centuries, water rich with sustenance, and yet water that is dark witness to those it carried away from this place and those it left behind who perished. You purse your lips and make a sound that starts off like river water and ends with the wash of river water against the shoals – a sound and name that mirror meaning – for Sligeach means "the place of shells," or "shelly river," a name thousands of years old. A name that commemorates both the river and the inhabitants who feasted on what those waters provided, a people who would create a language, lose it, resurrect and reclaim it. We know of them because they left a line of relics...in the form of discarded shells that fill the middens downwind of their ancient burial ground, and in their descendants who live there now, who have a history as old as time.

Grainne's End
an excerpt

Up in the hills above Sligo Town, in a cottage which decades later will become a boarding house for travelers, transients and street performers, the old woman, as bow-legged as the crook in the forked tree down in the graveyard at the foot of the hill, made her way to the hob. She was swift in spite of the rheumatism, and her twisted silhouette that loomed up beside the turf fire in the grate was a formidable one. Sure she'd be reading him the leaves in a little while, after the tea had steeped just enough for him to sip the hot brew; then it would be his fortune that would rise up out of the steam and the silt left behind.

He came here in the evenings, week after week, a gangly dark youth, in the darkness of night. He came for the stories about the odd remnants of human beings that inhabited these hills – farmers mostly, and fishermen present and past, the soothsayer and the dreamers – what there were of them – the young brides and even younger children stolen from the roads and never heard from again. The old woman was the keeper of their tales. Truth be told, he came here most for the talk of the other creatures. Some folks told him to stay away, that Bridey up in the hills was cousin to the *bean-si*, but he knew well enough that there were faery folk and there were real folk. Bridey for all her strangeness, he was fairly certain – though sometimes when he'd see her wandering the road down to the village in the moonlight going heaven knows where and he'd question this certitude – was one of the real.

Tonight, after the tales, and after she had roused to life once again the ancient Irish lovers Darmuid and Grainne who slept just outside across the way within the tomb of the mountain, she took the china cup from him and swirled the skeletons of its meager remains; then she held it before the flame. The dying fire provided the only light in the old cottage that was growing bitterly cold by the moment. Outside, the wind howled and the rain and snow continued to lash the trees and the path and the pale stone walls, turning everything inconsequential, and he began to wonder how he would make it down the hill to the town, but she told him to quiet his mind. She sat over the heavy white stone mug and peered down inside. A twisted version of the letter m clung to the rim, she said, and strive as she did to find an errant bird or an anchor beside the rogue letter, a stark few leaves clotted together and formed a tall and solitary tower instead.

She continued to look inside the mug for a long time, as if detecting in it, some finely tuned knowledge of what awaited him in the bloodlines of his ancestors, out on the roads beyond this cottage. And then she shook her head. He wanted to know what she saw in the incomprehensible pattern of the leaves, their drowned remains laid out where they had washed up on the shoreline of the ironstone vessel, but without looking back up at him, and with those eyes that changed color with the wind, she said it didn't matter. He was still young.

When he finally reached the town, the snow and sleet had left the streets deserted. The wind had pried loose the sign off the pub that faced the harbor so that it squeaked and tapped, squeaked and tapped a steady cadence against the edifice. He didn't stop here as he usually did, to peer into the dark waters and imagine the coffin ships filling. He didn't let the wailing women, the stiff-lipped men and the young folks hiding their tears as they boarded, enter his mind. They always seemed to call to him now from this place that was haunted with so much ache and loss. He'd never noticed this as a child, but they were out and about tonight, as he made his way up the street to his room.

The ghostwind howled across the open spaces and whistled through the burrow behind him, the blind men and the fiddlers hidden deep within the dark. The mills were silent tonight, and the abbey with its cloisters and tomb would be filling up with wet snow. The thought came to him that he could be the last man alive on earth.

He stood outside a moment longer looking across toward Knocknarea, the mountain that he loved. He didn't want to be alone this evening with the old woman troubling his thoughts, but this was not a night for friends; it was time to gather together his notes into some semblance of order, to document this latest installment and set down a coherent record for those who would come after, when everyone else up in the hills would be long asleep, their tales all but forgotten. Once back up in his room, in the amber light and the warmth of the fire in the grate, he sat at the small walnut desk and wrote.

Grainne, nearing the end

A chilling wind slithered down the slope where the two of them had agreed to hide that night. Night after night at this hour, she would begin to hear the wolves, begin to sense the nighthawks circling overhead, waiting to feast on their flesh, and she would want to shout, "Not yet. You'll have to wait yet, if you want us." Between dusk and dark, she would feel the shadows moving closer over the hills and she couldn't help but wonder if he had been worth it, but at midnight when they would lie in each other's arms, and he would make his way down that fine narrow path between her breasts and then circle and pull on her nipple with his fingers just before lovemaking, she could almost believe they would outlive the old giant who stalked them through dream and waking, but she knew their end was near...

That evening with its untold dreams of what lay ahead was suspended now in the amber of the past. Time had moved on, and another had taken its place. The old woman was long gone. Her stories still roamed the hillsides and made their way down to the loughs, still roamed the hills in his mind, too. Indeed, the old cottage had been turned over three, maybe four times by now, and had come to rest in a grand-niece's hands. She had added on to it and turned it into a boarding house. He knew all of this and kept an eye on the place, even now, but his time, like Bridey's, was long past. If anything stirred down in the churchyard beyond his empty stone marker, or in the mountain that loomed above it where the lovers slept, it wasn't for him to get involved. He had become in death just as he had anticipated – the opposite of who and what he had been in life. Pen and ink and paper were no more; poetry was no more; there was no more writing and rewriting, no more counting the measured verse in his head, or finding the perfect word that would ignite the spark in his readers' minds, or better, their hearts. Poems were for the living to write and to find, as was love. And while he should have stayed quiet and slept on in that eternal dream of the shades, he hadn't.

He had walked every one of these hills and the narrow threading streets of the town, he had strolled these quays alongside the river and had memorized every landmark – hills, waterfalls, faery-fort and wood, aristocratic houses and the rough hewn huts like Bridey's and the folks who turned the soil and kept the place alive, those who had come out of the bogs and had been driven back into them, welcomed in the end, by the earth that had nourished them.

Now, he was about to set out once more, a different purpose forming in his mind, a different rhyme scheme. His step quickened, as if he were young again. A new and numinous stanza about to write itself thrust him out into the kinetic night, along the Sligo roads.

Ogham *

In the old language
Tracks were inscribed
In Rock - even now
Millennia later, they ride
Skyward up the sides, across the tops
And course back down these standing rocks
As if guiding the long dead
Through unlit passages
To the earth they once plowed and planted

Stones, they tell us, received these
Earliest writings, and later,
Manuscripts, and secret messages
Were believed to have passed
Between participating parties

Political intrigue?
Religious survival?
First poems?

Theories exist
But still, we surmise

Stakes and wooden sticks were etched as well
And if we look across the channel, beyond the ocean
We might reach the verge where Yeats
        and his cousins gather in a clearing

And through our small-paned glass, see him
With his tablet
Making the ancient markings
Tracks
To the spirits of plant and tree
Stone and wood

The young poet intent on carving a path
Under the low-flying swans
Nearing dark

*The oldest remains of the Ancient Irish alphabet that appear on Memorial or
Standing stones from the 5th and 6th centuries

Arrival

Think of this place as one of those passages
Zola might have described, not darkly like his
Passage du Pont Neuf, but with that same eye to detail
And lit with uncharacteristic light

one that Time passes through and touches
and brings to life: bus depot, traffic

an old woman wrapped in wind
a pink windbreaker, and hair
the color of rust
and dust

a busy street where
Illusions abound, and

Language is breath

The rise and fall of
Mountain and river
Shadows crossing the quay

Imposing Knocknarea
            in its long
                        descent
                                into mist

the burnished end of a Sligo day

Columcille

We arrived here first
the towering Celtic Cross ebony
against the agate blue of Irish sky
wheeling high above us as we raised
our eyes to take it in
circle it, memorize its carvings
capture it in our secondary lens

The guide did his best
to fill us in, but it was late, he said
and we'd best be getting inside –
the church and graveyard waited

The High Cross remained behind

It extended its arms the way a child might
In welcome, or longing
                    to hold us a moment more

The sandstone High Cross which Yeats memorialized in "Under Ben Bulben," stands near the church and graveyard at Drumcliff. Drumcliff was originally a monastery founded in the 6th Century by St. Columcille or Columba.

A Famine Memorial
Sligo Bay and Knocknarea

How dark Knocknarea grows at times
While Maeve sleeps on in her silent cairn
To stand on this quay is to hear again
The ships moving out, the broken rhymes

Of poet, lover, mother, child
The clutching hands now forelost cities
The resolute men all without pity's
Stance; the women now rain-soaked and wild

Stand on this ground and sense the shift
The river's memory itself a grave
Both Charon and the shades' watery cave
As the young set forth coinless, adrift

The coffin ships sail, Death's crude mimes
On the wind, hear the ghosts' forlorn cries
Under Queen Maeve's ever silent eyes
How dark Knocknarea grows at times

Knocknarea - one of two major mountains in Sligo imbued with legend and folklore; believed by many to be the final resting place of Queen Maeve, queen of the Western Sidhe [the fairy people of Irish mythology, pronounced SHE]

cairn - a mound of stones marking a burial place

The Quay - where, at the height of the Famine, 27 ships set sail, one sinking just outside the harbor, in Sligo Bay... all of those aboard perished. Thousands of others died before reaching their destination.

Letter Home
on the phases and noted absence
of the moon

I

Here, in the west of Ireland
There is no moon
Ben Bulben and Knocknarea
And off beyond the tombs
Donegal's pale blue cliffs all rise
But the moon is missing and
I wonder do you have it
Up there in that tangled wood
Stitched between the music
    and the leaves, on the lake
        where you row out beyond
            the noise of the mind
                does it follow?

I grow distant here, lost
In a land of fairy forts and cairns
So vast, remote and alone
And yet, as if once, in some long ago
I might have been here
As leaf, heather, or stone
I could lie down
    and feel at home
        forever

Letter Home
on the phases and noted absence
of the moon

II

"I haven't been able to find the moon,"
she wrote him, in a letter she never sent
A man from Galway told her
he'd found it on the bus the night before
on the way up to his room
so she looked past the wild
disorder of his syntax
to see if it were still where he'd said
but the red of her hair had caught his eye
and her eye saw
that this was the land where magic was said
to roam the hills at night
and men like this with gold earrings and smiles
came and went through that vanishing door
where the doomed lovers
Diarmuid and Grainne slept

so she moved away and kept to herself
the memory of light

through the small storeroom door

At Glen Car Waterfall

Hear the waters of Glen Car
As they cascade down the rocks
The woods so full of whispers
As the sidhe undo the locks

As the sidhe undo their locks
In flashes of blue and white
Strangers in odd procession
Ascend the enchanted site

Ascending the ancient site
Each pilgrim, guide and tourist
Turns quiet in this thicket
Even the very poorest

Feels the hum of magic here
In the pure sun splashed waters
In covert, on wind-formed path
They tiptoe through these quarters

They tiptoe through these quarters
Where the sidhe can see afar
And yet choose to remain here
By the waters of Glen Car

The kaleidoscopic sky
Grows dark; every soul is caught
Between the world, a tumbler of wonder
And the heart, a fairy fort

Upon finding a chestnut tree
in a poem by Yeats

all night long in this hotel room
that has become my sanctuary
in this strange wondrous land
I read of the Irish poet and his love

walk the hills where he dreamt her
ghostly girl in a schoolroom
Leda's daughter, Sparta's queen

And on a summer breeze turned suddenly cold
He beckons to me
       come find the same wild blossoming,
       the same excess of woodland scent in rain

          the dancer in the dance
     the candleflame in leaf

Revenant
[a dream poem]

I come from a land
Where old men
With Anglo-Irish tongues
Speak haltingly ---
So low that your
Mind becomes an inn where strangers
Come at night, blown in with the leaves and
Something of the wind
        still clings
To the wool of their sweaters and scarves
You put up the tea and wonder
        at the lateness of the train
When one of these men

        white-haired and beautiful
        in that way they have
        of making you want to lean in and
        listen
        for aren't they all
        filled with tales

claims, "You see a certain woman
and want to make love…"

        and across the table
the tea and the train be damned
you wait… for this
is the restless, rustling one

the tale the morning birds forsake their crannies
        to perch on your sill and sing

In Sligo

Beside the waters of Glen Car spilling across the stones
In the gray and mist swept air and in the fern's sure fluted fronds
On the bridge that wasn't bridge at all, but floating climbing stair
I met you in those lush green woods. Yes, I met you there.

In the song that Martin sang as he took us up into the hills
Of faeries who stole a child from this world much too full of tears
And in the memory's banquet of such sweet contrasting fare
I met you again. Yes, I met you there.

And as those wild swans at evening, lifted off the page, and
The girl in the schoolroom altered, into dawn and then old age,
And the man made of this loss and love, a coat so rich and rare
I met you in time's early dusk. Yes, I met you there.

Among the megalithic stones, in the sweep of cliffs and moors
In tumbling white clouds of changing skies, in stone walls along the road
In the coverlet of stars one night spread out over all my cares
I met you. Yes. I met you everywhere.

at Keohane's Bookshop
on Castle Street

in the diligence of their conversation
the shop owner's and the scholar's
came a lull long enough to ask her question

but a book she was seeking
wasn't to be found
the last copy sold an hour before

the writer told her one would reach her
when she reached home
and then he called her by name
her other name, the one she never shared

they spoke of Massine, and fairy tales
and dancing beyond the hourglass's sand
the commerce of shadows
in the mottled dark
and when he was called away
they said goodbye

even now
in that empty space that once housed
a kingdom of books and untold treasures
the conversations continue

it is why we should always respect
the places-in-between

the ones we believe don't exist anymore

for George Watson

Yeats's Grave
[perceptions]

I

the place they took us to
before the first word
could be uttered

II

through the twilight
Ben Bulben
rising like a blue dream
in the attic of the landscape

III

Shhh...
Diarmuid and Grainne
are whispering behind their
limestone door

IV

where his feet once stood
a pot of forlorn flowers
foretells the tale to come

V

windy ghostland
who walks among these stones at night?

Yeats in the Underworld
On a Sunday Morning, Riding the Uptown #2

What does it matter
Where they lay the bones
The man was a man
Only a man some would say
But others, everywhere, an Excess
A man who could never be contained

So, why the surprise
What matter the pot of flowers
The pomp at the re-graving, the
Engraving in stone
   the runes, the hieroglyphs, the fairies,
    the dawn and the gold

Even this morning, five years after the certainty
Could no longer make room for doubt, they had to admit
The great man's bones
   are not in that plot in Drumcliff

He appeared this morning in the tunnels
On the platform of the Uptown 2, a wind blew in
And with it the trilling of birds, like those that
   sometimes make their way down out of the cold above ground
    on a winter's day

There was no mistaking him –
   the towering height
   the silver hair combed in just that way
   the horn-rimmed glasses
   on the patrician nose

He strode over to where I stood, as the train pulled in,
Stepped in and sat down beside me
That's when I decided to put all of this down

What does it matter where they lay the bones...

The Other, Darker Side
because the story can never be wished away
and never be half-told

It was not all grace and beauty or
Celtic twilight, night after night

Sirens went off, and shells
And the wail and walls that would be
Erected and torn down
Smeared with the blood of the lost

And then there was the lull we were told
But we know that life, though not death,
Is far more
Complex than that

For too long *Longing* has been lodged in
The stones and stony walls
And hearts of this land

Where mothers and lovers
Are destined to draw their shrouds about them
And bury their dead

Stand up and speak out if words still
Hold any currency against the dark
The cycle he warned of
Had already begun years before, but

The fires still burn
They climb the throats of the stunned

for Lyra McKee
March 31, 1990 – April 18, 2019
and for Sara Canning

Legacy
Inspired by two words of the poet

here, in the space that is neither
space nor matter, the thought comes
as if on a wind that blows in
off the sea, this end of summer evening

that the hand held over time
or held in myriad ways
over the course of a life

creates a form of dwelling itself

like those stone houses
along the west coast
of Ireland
remote and brave against the storm swells
of unforgiving seas
this cabin holds warmth
within

and secrets

a turf fire glows
in the dark and shadowed places of the night
and the cold windy light when just a glimmer
of morning is stirring
the waking hills
enters

always there is that soft strewn
spilling over light

for Eavan Boland

from Beginnings,
a final thought

the once upon a time
that no one today ever knew
      was a time of place

of windy promontories
and abbeys that rose up
out of the sea
not markets or colorful bazaars
but cliffs of dazzling heights
and birds made
moonstone by the rocky north Atlantic light

and yet, where does this enter a life
what value to have come from these
if all we have ever known and loved
is city life
with its chiaroscuro of falling light and shadow
its millions of neighbors
its tugboats and rivers, barrios
and bridges, its reeling
and... its *realing*

out there in the ancient night
our unvoiced question receives its answer
like church bells that toll the hours
the whistle's lament travels
through space and distant stars

it reminds us
that something or someone
even now, is listening
calling to us from the dark...

that the once upon a time
the once that is no more

      is

in the cell, like protoplasm
or gold

Helen Morrissey Rizzuto, author of *Evening Sky on a Japanese Screen*, *A Bird in Flight*, *In the dark curfew'd streets... Long Beach, Long Island in the aftermath*, *The Lenten Moon* and co-author of *American By Choice – One Man's Journey*, is an award-winning poet and fiction writer. She has taught at Hofstra University and Queens College, and for New York State Council on the Arts, as a resident poet and author.

Presently, she conducts private workshops in poetry, fiction, character, and Ekphrasis and the Illustrated Journal, both in New York City and on Long Island. Her students have gone on to win prestigious prizes from Random House, Little, Brown and Co. and other major publishing houses.

She can be contacted at helenmorrisseyrizzuto@gmail.com

This edition of
Helen Morrissey Rizzuto's
In the Old Language...following the path of the Poet
was designed by Grace Maher Graphic Design

www.gracemaher.com

The text is set in Stempel Garamond LT Standard